Math All Around

Money at the Store

Jennifer Rozines Roy and Gregory Roy

Marshall Cavendish
Benchmark
New York

We're going to make ice cream sundaes!
But we don't have any ice cream or toppings.
Let's go shopping!

At the grocery store we grab a cart. We take out our shopping list. It shows all the things we need to buy today.

Shopping list:

vanilla ice cream

ice cream toppings

two bananas

whipped cream

Looks like we know *what* to buy. But how will we buy it? With money, of course! We'll use money — and math — to be super shoppers!

Open your wallet. Let's see how much money is inside. Forty-one cents. That's not very much. We'll have to stop at the **Automatic Teller Machine (ATM)**.

Pop in the ATM card and punch in your secret code. The machine sends a message to the bank, and subtracts money from your bank account.

A twenty-dollar bill comes out. How will we know if this is enough money to buy everything on our list? And how will we keep track of how much we are spending? We can't spend more than $20.41.

We'll use a **calculator** and our math smarts!

Welcome to the **produce aisle**. Look at all the fruits and vegetables! They come in different colors, shapes, and sizes.

Money comes in different colors, shapes, and sizes, too. Coins are round pieces of metal.

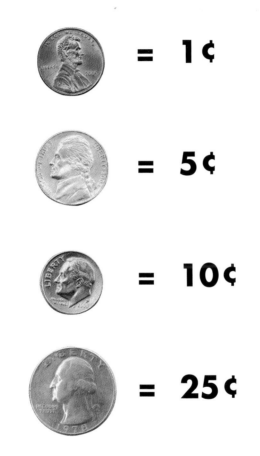

= 1 ¢

= 5 ¢

= 10 ¢

= 25 ¢

There's one of each coin in your wallet!

You can buy single bananas off the bunch for twenty-five cents each. That could be one quarter, or five nickels, or two dimes and five pennies.

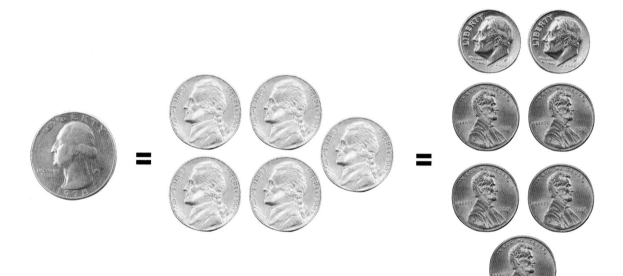

But we don't pay until we check out. Just drop two of the bananas in the cart. Now let's start adding up the money!

One banana is twenty-five cents. But to enter it into the calculator, we'll need to type it a different way.

An amount of money can be written with a dot called a **decimal point** (**.**). The number of cents is written *after* the decimal point.

So type in **.25** for twenty-five cents for one banana. But there are two bananas! So press the plus sign (**+**) to add and type in **.25** again.

Now press the equal sign (**=**) to find out how much we've spent so far. Fifty cents or **.50**.

We'll add each price into the calculator. That way we can keep track of how much we've spent.

Cross the bananas off the list, and let's move on.

Shopping list:

vanilla ice cream

ice cream toppings

~~two bananas~~

whipped cream

Aisle two is the candy aisle. We can get our sundae toppings here. The sign says $2.99 each.

We know that the numbers *after* the decimal point are the cents—ninety-nine cents.

The number *before* the decimal point means dollars—two dollars.

One dollar equals 100 cents.

 =

or

or

or

If we didn't have dollar bills, we would have to carry a lot of coins around the store. They would be heavy *and* noisy!

Dollars are paper money that come in different amounts.

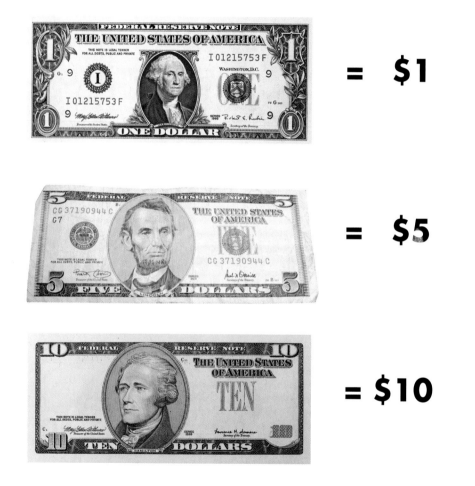

= $1

= $5

= $10

   =   **$20**

   =   **$50**

=   **$100**

Of course, you've seen a twenty-dollar bill. You have one in your wallet! That gives us plenty of money to buy sprinkles, hot fudge, and chocolate chips.

We've added four toppings to our cart. Each topping was $2.99.

Now we'll add their prices to the price of the bananas. Enter **2.99 + 2.99 + 2.99 + 2.99** into the calculator. Press the equal sign. That shows how much things cost so far.

We're up to **$12.46**.
We have $20.41 in the wallet,
so we can keep shopping!

In the freezer section, we look at all the ice cream. How will we choose just one?

We want vanilla. But different companies make different **brands**. Let's look at these three brands and their prices.

If we were just trying to save money today, we'd choose the third one. It's the cheapest.

But that ice cream doesn't taste as good as the others. So saving money this time won't be worth it.

The first ice cream is too small and fancy for our sundaes. It also costs the most money.

So we'll buy the second ice cream. Place it in the cart and type **(+) 3.19** into the calculator. Next press the equal sign. We're up to **$15.65**. Now let's finish our shopping, so the ice cream doesn't melt!

Shopping list:

~~vanilla ice cream~~

~~ice cream toppings~~

~~two bananas~~

whipped cream

In the **dairy aisle**, we stop in front of the whipped cream. Should we get the kind in the tub that you spoon out? Or should we buy the one in the squirt can?

We pick the squirty kind. It's on **sale**. A sale means that the store is selling something at a lower price. Cross it off the list!

Add **2.15** for the whipped cream to our total. Let's check what we are up to now. Press the equal sign. **$17.80**!

We have everything on our list. Let's check out our items.

The **cashier** rings up all of our treats. They add up to $17.80, just like we figured out on the calculator.

Give the twenty-dollar bill to the cashier. She gives you back $2.20.

The difference between $20.00 and $17.80 is $2.20. Put your change back in the wallet. That was smart shopping!

Our super shopping trip is over, and now it's time to eat!

Money paid for our groceries. Math helped us buy the right things at the right price.

Grab a spoon. Delicious!

Glossary

Automatic Teller Machine (ATM) — A computerized machine that electronically connects to banks so customers can take out and put in money.

brand — A name that a company gives the things it sells.

calculator — A machine that can solve math problems.

cashier — The person you pay when you buy something at a store.

dairy aisle — The section of a supermarket that has milk, cream, butter, and cheese.

decimal point — A period, or dot (.), that separates dollars from cents.

produce aisle — The section of a supermarket that has fruits and vegetables.

sale — Selling something for a lower price.

Read More

Axelrod, Amy. *Pigs Go to Market: Fun with Math and Shopping*. Aladdin, 1999.

Leedy, Loreen. *The Monster Money Book*. Holiday House, 2000.

Murphy, Stuart J. *Sluggers' Car Wash*. HarperCollins, 2002.

Web Sites

AAAKnow Math: Consumer Math
www.aaaknow.com/mny.htm

Funbrain: Change Maker
www.funbrain.com/cashreg/index.html

Teach R Kids Math
www.teachrkids.com/

Index

Page numbers in **boldface** are illustrations.

adding. *See* calculator
Automatic Teller Machine (ATM), 4, **4**

bananas, 8–9, **9**
bank account, 4
brands, **19**, 19–21, **20**, **21**

calculator, 5, **5**, **10**, 10–11, 12,
    16–17, **17**, 21, 22, **22**, 23, **23**
candy aisle, 12, **12**
cashier, 24–25
cents, 4, 10, 12, **13**
    See also coins
change, 25, **25**
checkout, 9, **24**, 24–25
coins, **7**, 7–8, **8**, 13, **13**

dairy aisle, 22
decimal point, 10, 12
dimes, **7**, **13**
dollars, 12–13, **13**
    See also paper money

equal sign, 10

freezer section, 18, **18**

ice cream, **18**, **19**, 19–21
    20, **21**
ice cream sundaes, 3, **27**

keeping track, 10

nickels, **7**, **13**

on sale, 22
one dollar, 13, **13**, **14**

paper money, **5**, **13**, 13–15, **14**, **15**
paying, 9, **24**, 24–25
pennies, **7**, **13**
prices, comparing, **19**, 19–21, **21**, 22, 26
produce aisle, 6, **6**

quarters, 8, **8**, **13**

shopping list, **3**, **11**, **21**, **23**

toppings, 12, 16, **16**

whipped cream, **22**, 22–23

About the Authors

Jennifer Rozines Roy is the author of more than twenty books. A former Gifted and Talented teacher, she holds degrees in psychology and elementary education.

Gregory Roy is a civil engineer who has co-authored several books with his wife. The Roys live in upstate New York with their son Adam.

Marshall Cavendish Benchmark
99 White Plains Road
Tarrytown, New York 10591-9001
www.marshallcavendish.us

Library of Congress Cataloging-in-Publication Data

Roy, Jennifer Rozines, 1967–
Money at the store : by Jennifer Rozines Roy & Gregory Roy.
p. cm. — (Math all around)
Summary: "Reinforces both budgeting and calculator skills, stimulates critical thinking,
and provides students with an understanding of math in the real world"—Provided by publisher.
Includes index.
ISBN-13: 978-0-7614-2264-8
ISBN-10: 0-7614-2264-1
1. Counting—Juvenile literature. 2. Money—Juvenile literature. 3. Shopping—Juvenile literature.
4. Mathematics—Study and teaching (Elementary)—Juvenile literature. I. Roy, Gregory. II. Title.
III. Series: Roy, Jennifer Rozines, 1967– Math all around.
QA113.R69 2006
513.2'11—dc22
2006009169

Photo Research by Anne Burns Images

Cover Photo by *Jay Mallin Photos*

The photographs in this book are used with permission and through the courtesy of:
Jay Mallin Photos: pp. 1, 2, 4, 5B, 7(all), 8(all), 10, 11, 12, 13R, 14C, 16(all), 17, 18, 19(all), 20(all), 21, 22, 23, 24, 25b, 27.
Getty Images: pp. 5T, 15T&C, 20T&C. *Corbis*: p. 6 Mark E. Gibson; pp. 13L, 14T, 15B, 25T Joseph Sohm;
Visions of America; p. 14B Reuters. *Superstock*: p. 9 Ingram Publishing.

Series design by Virginia Pope

Printed in Malaysia
1 3 5 6 4 2